THE NEW YOU

by
Andrew Wommack

Unless otherwise indicated, all Scripture quotations are taken from the *King James Version* of the Bible.

The New You
ISBN 1-59548-054-4
Copyright © 2005 by Andrew Wommack Ministries, Inc.
850 Elkton Dr.
Colorado Springs, CO 80907

Published by Andrew Wommack Ministries, Inc.

Printed in the United States of America. All rights reserved under International Copyright Law. Contents and/or cover may not be reproduced in whole or in part in any form without the express written consent of the Andrew Wommack Ministries, Inc.

TABLE OF CONTENTS

Introduction

Part I

Born Again

Choosing to receive Jesus Christ as your Lord and Savior is the most important decision you'll ever make. This book will help you understand the choice you've made and discover what's next.

Welcome to the family!

Introduction
Part II

Loving God

Now that you're born again, what's next?

God wants to establish some new patterns in your life. By taking the following "first steps" with Him, you'll lay a solid foundation for a growing relationship.

God's love for you won't change whether you do these things or not, but your love for Him will definitely be affected! You've been given the gift of a brand-new life, full of untold potential that's just waiting to be developed. Why settle for anything less than your divine destiny?

Fall deeply in love with God—He's worth it!

Chapter 1

Understand Your Salvation

When God's Word first comes to you, Satan immediately tries to steal it (Matt.13:19). However, he can only do so if you don't understand. That's why you need to comprehend what takes place the moment you accept the Lord. Understanding prevents the devil from talking you out of your salvation benefits.

God's Word promises **"that if thou shalt confess with thy mouth the Lord Jesus, and shalt believe in thine heart that God hath raised him from the dead, thou shalt be saved. For with the heart man believeth unto righteousness; and with the mouth confession is made unto salvation"** (Rom. 10:9-10). **"For whosoever shall call upon the name of the Lord shall be saved"** (Rom. 10:13).

Have you done this? Have you confessed with your mouth the Lord Jesus? Do you believe in your heart God raised Him from the dead? Are you a "whosoever" who has called on the name of the Lord? If your answer is yes, then you've been saved!

You were saved the very moment you sincerely committed your life to Jesus Christ. The truth of His Word instantly came to pass as you believed in your heart and confessed with your mouth. Congratulations, you've been saved!

God Keeps His Word

You're in good hands now! **"I give unto them eternal life; and they shall never perish, neither shall any man pluck them out of my hand. My Father, which gave them me, is greater than all; and no man is able to pluck them out of my Father's hand"** (John 10:28-29).

Since you've committed your life to Him, He'll keep you. **"For the which cause I also suffer these things: nevertheless I am not ashamed: for I know whom I have believed, and am persuaded that he is able to keep that which I have committed unto him against that day"** (2 Tim. 1:12).

God will be faithful even when you aren't! **"It is a faithful saying: For if we be dead with him, we shall**

also live with him: If we suffer, we shall also reign with him: if we deny him, he also will deny us: If we believe not, yet he abideth faithful: he cannot deny himself" (2 Tim. 2:11-13). When you make mistakes or feel discouraged—just remember, God can't deny Himself, because He always keeps His Word!

Knowledge Unlocks Experience

Knowledge from God's Word helps you comprehend what took place in your life at salvation. You began an eternal relationship with the most Wonderful Person in the universe. Knowing and following Him will bring you unspeakable joy. Salvation isn't just going to heaven when you die; God wants you to start experiencing your salvation benefits immediately. This requires knowledge from His Word. As you understand and act on that knowledge, you'll experience the benefits of your salvation.

God has given you everything you need for life and godliness through the knowledge of Him. **"Grace and peace be multiplied unto you through the knowledge of God, and of Jesus our Lord, According as his divine power hath given unto us all things that pertain unto life and godliness, through the knowledge of him that hath called us to glory and virtue: Whereby are given unto us exceeding great and precious promises: that by these ye might be partakers of the divine nature, having escaped the corruption that is in the world through lust"** (2 Pet. 1:2-4). The knowledge of God gives you access to His promises. By believing and acting on them, you'll partake of His divine nature. This means you'll experience all of God's love, joy, peace, health, deliverance, prosperity, and so on that's already in your spirit now by Christ Jesus!

As your thinking changes to line up with your born-again spirit, your life will too. For instance, perhaps you've spent your entire life hating Mondays. You've always given it over to the devil by believing, speaking, and expecting it to be a bad day. Just because you were born again doesn't mean that all of your negative attitudes and thought patterns have changed yet. Monday will be the same as before until knowledge from God's Word causes you to understand and act differently toward it. As the Word changes the way you believe, speak, and expect things to be, you'll start experiencing your salvation benefits—even on Mondays!

Renew Your Mind!

Your whole outlook will change as you grow in the knowledge of God and His promises. This is called "renewing your mind." **"I beseech you therefore, brethren, by the mercies of God, that ye present your bodies a living sacrifice, holy, acceptable unto God, which is your reasonable service. And be not conformed to this world: but be ye transformed by the renewing of your mind, that ye may prove what is that good, and acceptable, and perfect, will of God"** (Rom. 12:1-2).

You must change the way you think to match your born-again spirit. At salvation, your spirit became an entirely new creation. **"Therefore if any man be in Christ, he is a new creature: old things are passed away; behold, all things are become new"** (2 Cor. 5:17). Your born-again spirit is always in agreement with God. The Word will renew your mind to what's already happened in your spirit.

God wants you to think and act like Him! By submitting yourself to His Word, your life will change like a caterpillar transforms into a beautiful butterfly. Don't allow worldly pressure to squeeze you into its ungodly mold by failing to renew your mind. Instead, be transformed by the knowledge of God, and your life will increasingly reflect Christ Jesus.

Your Spirit Changed

Some people don't understand the spiritual nature of the radical change that occurred when they committed their lives to Christ. For example, many individuals receive Jesus in jail, because they're desperate for a change. Waking up the next morning, they find themselves in the same cell, wearing the same clothes, and eating the same food. They don't feel any different, and their circumstances certainly haven't changed. Discouraged by this lack of immediate outward transformation, they incorrectly conclude that nothing really happened at all. Because of this, many never go on to renew their minds and enjoy the benefits of their salvation.

Your body and soul (mind, will, and emotions) didn't change at salvation the way your spirit did. If you were fat before being born again, you were fat afterward. If you were bad at math before you got saved, you'll stay bad at math until you increase in learning. Your mind isn't instantly changed. It's your spirit that's been made new!

Since you can't see or touch your spirit, God's Word is the only way you can know for sure what has happened within. **"It is the spirit that quickeneth; the flesh profiteth nothing: the words that I speak unto you, they are spirit, and they are life"** (John 6:63). Faith is simply trusting what the Word says happened in your spirit more than what you see in the natural.

Trust the Truth

When I accepted the Lord as an eight-year-old, all I experienced was an inward "knowing." A nagging fear of hell left, but other than that, nothing felt different to me. There were no bells, no whistles, nor fireworks. I had to believe God's Word that my salvation was true. As I renewed my mind, I increasingly partook of His divine nature and enjoyed living in His promises.

Feelings change, but the truth doesn't! If you genuinely committed your life to the Lord, the truth is He will always honor that commitment. He'll never deny, leave, nor forsake you (Matt.10:32, Heb. 13:5). Your relationship with God is secure. Whether you felt anything or not, radical change took place in your spirit, and you're now a brand-new person. Trust that God's Word to you is true!

You'll experience your salvation more as you renew your mind. When you think according to the flesh (i.e., what your five senses tell you) and give in to negative external influences, you won't be able to enjoy God's benefits. However, as you trust the truth of God's Word by keeping your mind on the Lord and thinking in line with your born-again spirit, you'll experience God's love, peace, joy, etc. (Gal. 5:22-23). The choice is yours. Begin renewing your mind today!

Chapter 2

Jesus Is Lord

Salvation is God's gift to you through faith in Jesus Christ. **"For the wages of sin is death; but the gift of God is eternal life through Jesus Christ our Lord"** (Rom. 6:23). Salvation can't be earned by any amount of good works, because God doesn't give eternal life based on anything you do. Jesus Christ did everything that needed to be done through His death, burial, and resurrection. You receive eternal life by faith in Him alone!

No one deserves to be saved because of their good works. **"For all have sinned, and come short of the glory of God"** (Rom. 3:23). God doesn't deal with you in proportion to your sin. If you miss heaven by an inch, then you've missed it by a mile. Either you are completely righteous in His sight or you're not. It's that simple! No matter how good you think you are, you've been bad enough to miss heaven!

The Lord explicitly stated that He's not just ***a*** way to the Father, but ***the*** way! **"Jesus saith unto him, I am the way, the truth, and the life: no man cometh unto the Father, but by me"** (John 14:6). Acts 4:12 declares, **"Neither is there salvation in any other: for there is none other name under heaven given among men, whereby we must be saved."** Either you come to God the Father through faith in His Son Jesus Christ, or you don't come at all!

God in the Flesh

"And when he was gone forth into the way, there came one running, and kneeled to him, and asked him, Good Master, what shall I do that I may inherit eternal life? And Jesus said unto him, Why callest thou me good? there is none good but one, that is, God. Thou knowest the commandments, Do not commit adultery, Do not kill, Do not steal, Do not bear false witness, Defraud not, Honour thy father and mother. And he answered and said unto him, Master, all these have I observed from my youth" (Mark 10:17-20).

A rich young ruler asked Jesus, "What must I do to inherit eternal life?" He wanted to know how he could earn his way into heaven. Notice how the young man called Jesus

"Good Master" at first. When the Lord countered him saying that only God is good, he dropped "Good" and referred to Jesus simply as "Master." By this we know he didn't see Jesus as God.

Jesus Christ was God in the flesh. He wasn't just a good man who gave us a tremendous example of humility and love. He was literally God incarnate! **"And without controversy great is the mystery of godliness: God was manifest in the flesh, justified in the Spirit, seen of angels, preached unto the Gentiles, believed on in the world, received up into glory"** (1 Tim. 3:16).

Either Jesus was a deceiver, or He is who He said He was. No man who claimed to be God as often and as openly as Jesus did—but wasn't—should ever be considered "good." However, there's more verifiable historical evidence proving that Jesus Christ lived, died, ***and*** was resurrected than that Julius Caesar ever lived!

Every cult and religion on earth acknowledges Jesus' existence, but stop short of calling Him God. They'll grant Him the status of a prophet or an inspired teacher sent from God, but not Deity Himself. The rich young ruler did the same by dropping "Good" and calling Jesus "Master." He just couldn't bring himself to believe that this Man standing before him was God.

Apart from Jesus being the Son of God, there's no way to the Father! Everything hinges on His divinity. The Lord Himself stated **"that all men should honour the**

Son, even as they honour the Father. He that honoureth not the Son honoureth not the Father which hath sent him" (John 5:23). If Jesus wasn't God, then His life wasn't worth more than any other man's life, and He couldn't have atoned for the whole human race. However, since He was God in the flesh, His life was worth more than all mankind—making His sacrifice eternally sufficient for all!

The Great Exchange

Christianity is the only faith with a Savior. All others depend on good works to achieve various degrees of "holiness." The holier you live, the better chance you have of being accepted by that "god." In essence, you become your own savior, because "salvation" is based on your own performance. God knew you couldn't live a perfect life! Instead of demanding that you do everything right, He came and took your sin into His own body at the cross (1 Pet. 2:24). He suffered the punishment you deserved, to give you salvation as a gift. Praise God for the Savior!

Jesus took your sin so you could become righteous! **"For he hath made him to be sin for us, who knew no sin; that we might be made the righteousness of God in him"** (2 Cor. 5:21). God put His judgment for sin upon Christ at the cross so you wouldn't have to bear it. Then, when you believed and received the Lord, He placed Jesus' righteousness on you. This is the Great Exchange!

When this exchange takes place, your spirit is immediately re-created with the righteousness of Jesus Christ. You are then able to fellowship with God spirit to Spirit. **"God is a Spirit: and they that worship him must worship him in spirit and in truth"** (John 4:24). Even when you sin, your born-again spirit cannot be contaminated, because of the impenetrable seal of Christ's own Spirit. **"In whom ye also trusted, after that ye heard the word of truth, the gospel of your salvation: in whom also after that ye believed, ye were sealed with that holy Spirit of promise"** (Eph. 1:13). Since the new nature of your spirit is always holy, you can approach God at any time and in any condition. Now that's good news!

Sustained by Faith

The Christian life is both born in faith and sustained by faith. You'll just end up condemning yourself if you try to live it by your own works. As long as you're in your physical body, there'll be times when you fall short. If you're not careful, you'll beat yourself up trying to live right and wonder how God could ever love someone who messes up as much as you.

God's love doesn't change when you make mistakes. If He went to the cross for you as a sinner, how much more does He love you now that you're a Christian! **"But God commendeth his love toward us, in that, while we were yet sinners, Christ died for us. Much more then, being now justified by his blood, we shall be saved from wrath through him. For if, when we were enemies, we were**

reconciled to God by the death of his Son, much more, being reconciled, we shall be saved by his life" (Rom. 5:8-10). He loves you more now as a Christian—even when you sin—than He did when you were lost. Don't ever let your failures separate you from God's unfailing love!

The Law's Purpose

God gave the Law to show mankind they couldn't save themselves. The "Ten Commandments" are really just the tip of the iceberg. There are literally thousands of rules to keep in the Law! Jesus used several of these commandments in an attempt to show the rich young ruler we read about in Mark 10 that he would never be holy enough for eternal life on his own. **"Thou knowest the commandments, Do not commit adultery, Do not kill, Do not steal, Do not bear false witness, Defraud not, Honour thy father and mother"** (Mark 10:19). This young man genuinely thought he could do something to earn eternal life. Doing and receiving by faith are very different from each other indeed!

The Law is like a plate glass window. Whether you break it with a BB or a boulder—it's broken! **"For whosoever shall keep the whole law, and yet offend in one point, he is guilty of all"** (James 2:10). God doesn't tell you to do your best and He'll make up the difference with mercy. Either you live holy and receive eternal life because you earned it (not possible), or you receive it by faith as a gift.

This deceived young ruler needed to quit trying and start trusting. In an effort to convince the Lord that he deserved eternal life, he told Jesus that he'd kept all of the commandments since his youth. Impossible! This man's attitude had him going straight to hell!

Loving the young ruler, Jesus tried to bring him out of this deception. **"Then Jesus beholding him loved him, and said unto him, One thing thou lackest: go thy way, sell whatsoever thou hast, and give to the poor, and thou shalt have treasure in heaven: and come, take up the cross, and follow me. And he was sad at that saying, and went away grieved: for he had great possessions"** (Mark 10:21-22). The Lord touched this man's true "god" when He instructed him to sell all of his possessions and give to the poor. The rich young ruler wasn't willing to lay them down and make Jesus Lord, because he'd broken the very first command—**"Thou shalt have no other gods before me"** (Ex. 20:3).

God is not against you having money, but He's against money having you! Giving away all of your possessions to the poor is not a requirement for salvation. When Zacchaeus, another wealthy man, met Jesus and repented, he declared he'd give half of all he had to the poor (Luke 19:1-9). Jesus never asked him to do it, but Zacchaeus volunteered to because his heart had changed. The issue Jesus is driving at is who or what do you trust in as your "god"/God?

The Bottom Line

If you believe Jesus Christ was only a good person and you can get to God through many different ways, then you haven't truly made Him Lord of your life yet. Jesus is either Lord of all, or He isn't Lord at all! You can't receive salvation, which comes only through Him, if you aren't willing to bow your knee and acknowledge Him as God and Supreme Ruler. Either Jesus Christ is your Savior ***and*** Lord, or He's not. It's that simple!

Chapter 3

From Death to Life

All people are born into this world separated from God (Ps. 51:5). Adam and Eve died spiritually when they sinned. Even though they didn't die physically right away, their spirits were separated from God and fell under the control of Satan (Gen. 3). Every person born into the earth since then has had this inherent sin nature. **"Wherefore, as by one man sin entered into the world, and death by sin; and so death passed upon all men, for that all have sinned"** (Rom. 5:12).

However, sin isn't imputed until you reach the age of accountability. This means you aren't held responsible for your sin until you're old enough to intentionally violate God's Law (Rom. 7:9). This age varies from person to person, but you need to be born again as soon as possible once you reach it.

A natural birth brought you into this world, but a spiritual birth is required to enter God's kingdom. **"Jesus answered and said unto him, Verily, verily, I say unto thee, Except a man be born again, he cannot see the kingdom of God. Nicodemus saith unto him, How can a man be born when he is old? can he enter the second time into his mother's womb, and be born? Jesus answered, Verily, verily, I say unto thee, Except a man be born of water and of the Spirit, he cannot enter into the kingdom of God"** (John 3:3-5).

When you're born again, you pass from death to life. **"Verily, verily, I say unto you, He that heareth my word, and believeth on him that sent me, hath everlasting life, and shall not come into condemnation; but is passed from death unto life"** (John 5:24). At salvation, the sin nature you were born with dies and is replaced with a brand-new, righteous nature. You're no longer a sinner but righteous in Christ!

Never Again!

God's standard of goodness is His own glory. You might have looked good compared to other sinners, but no one is holy compared to Jesus! According to Romans 3:23, **"For all have sinned, and come short of the glory of God."** Who wants to be the best sinner who ever went to hell? We all need a Savior. God declared everyone a sinner, but He loved us and wanted to redeem us. And in doing so, He could declare everyone righteous who has accepted Jesus by faith. Regardless of how bad you were, you instantly became righteous through receiving Christ.

Born-again Christians know they don't deserve salvation based on their own merits. It's only because they put faith in Jesus Christ and His finished work on the cross. All other religions try to approach God based on their personal holiness—what they do for Him. Christians approach God based on a firm heart belief in what He did for us.

All of your sins were forgiven—past, present, and future—the moment you received the Lord. You are now eternally redeemed and have an eternal inheritance (Heb. 9-10). In your spirit, you became sanctified and perfected in God's sight forever. **"To the general assembly and church of the firstborn, which are written in heaven, and to God the Judge of all, and to the spirits of just men made perfect"** (Heb. 12:23). Sin will never be imputed to you (credited to your account) again!

Choose Life!

Even though you're completely forgiven, it matters how you live! You have an Enemy who is committed to your destruction. **"The thief cometh not, but for to steal, and to kill, and to destroy: I am come that they might have life, and that they might have it more abundantly"** (John 10:10). The choices you make determine whether you experience life or death. **"Know ye not, that to whom ye yield yourselves servants to obey, his servants ye are**

to whom ye obey; whether of sin unto death, or of obedience unto righteousness" (Rom. 6:16). Yield to sin and you're yielding to the one whose revealed purpose is to steal, kill, and destroy you. Sin gives the devil a foothold in your life, and he'll take full advantage of it!

If you sin, simply repent. God will never leave you nor forsake you. He's already forgiven you, so don't fall for the deception that He doesn't love you or that you'll lose your salvation. God the Father already rejected and judged Jesus so you wouldn't have to be rejected and judged. Change your mind and turn from the sin. Declare, "Satan, I rebuke you. The blood of Jesus has set me free. Even though I didn't do what was right, you cannot destroy me. God loves me, and I choose to follow Him!" This prevents Satan from gaining entrance into your life.

Don't let the devil take advantage of you by you ignoring the way God shows you to live. Renew your mind to His Word, and act on it in faith. The abundant life Jesus provided is yours to enjoy!

For further study, I recommend my teaching *Spirit, Soul & Body.*

Chapter 4

Be Baptized

Every born-again believer should be baptized in water. This isn't in order to be saved but rather because you've been saved. **"Know ye not, that so many of us as were baptized into Jesus Christ were baptized into his death? Therefore we are buried with him by baptism into death: that like as Christ was raised up from the dead by the glory of the Father, even so we also should walk in newness of life"** (Rom. 6:3-4). Water baptism is an act of obedience to God's Word, symbolizing your baptism into the body of Christ.

You were immediately placed into the universal church upon your salvation. As a believer in Christ Jesus, you became part of His eternal body. **"There is one body, and one Spirit, even as ye are called in one hope of your calling; One Lord, one faith, one baptism, One God**

and Father of all, who is above all, and through all, and in you all" (Eph. 4:4-6). You became a part of every believer who has ever believed on the Lord Jesus Christ. It doesn't matter if they go to your local church, believe exactly the same as you or not; you've been united with all the other believers in the body of Christ!

God's Word commands you to be baptized in water. **"And he said unto them, Go ye into all the world, and preach the gospel to every creature. He that believeth and is baptized shall be saved; but he that believeth not shall be damned"** (Mark 16:15-16). **"Go ye therefore, and teach all nations, baptizing them in the name of the Father, and of the Son, and of the Holy Ghost"** (Matt. 28:19).

Numerous examples from the book of Acts show how the early church spread the Gospel and obeyed this command. On the Day of Pentecost, those who were saved were water baptized (Acts 2:41). Philip water baptized the Ethiopian eunuch and the new converts in Samaria (Acts 8). Thus, the scriptural pattern given for us to follow today is baptism of new believers by immersion in water.

Being "baptized" as a child in a religious system where they sprinkled you with water is not sufficient. Also, you weren't scripturally baptized if it was done prior to your true conversion (i.e., as an infant or young child). The Bible makes it very clear that faith in Jesus is a prerequisite to baptism (Acts 8:36-37). You must believe ***first*** and ***then*** be water baptized.

A Sign of Salvation

Although water baptism is an important first step in the Christian life, it's not required for salvation. Those who teach that water baptism is necessary to obtain your salvation are basing this on a misinterpretation of Acts 2:38. **"Then Peter said unto them, Repent, and be baptized every one of you in the name of Jesus Christ for the remission of sins, and ye shall receive the gift of the Holy Ghost."** Some say this "proves" you must repent ***and*** be baptized for the remission of sins. The key to understanding this verse is the word *for*. *For* often means "in order to obtain" but can also be "as a result of; because of; since." This verse says to repent, which means to put your faith in the Lord, and then to prove your faith in Him—*as a result* of being born again, *because* you've been born again, *since* you've been born again—by being water baptized. Those who believe that water baptism is required for salvation also teach that you must live in a system of religious works whereby you earn salvation by personal holiness. This is contrary to what the Word of God teaches as a whole.

Water baptism is a sign of salvation. In Acts 10, God told Cornelius through an angel to send for Peter in Joppa. When Peter came to Caesarea and began preaching to this man's entire household, they all received the baptism in the Holy Spirit, spoke in tongues, and prophesied. In light of this, Peter asked, "Can any man forbid water, that these should not be baptized?" In other words, they were born again, had received the Holy Spirit, and then were baptized in water (verses 44-48). Water baptism symbolized the salvation they had already received.

Holy Spirit Baptism

Once you are born again and water baptized, your very next step should be to receive the power of the Holy Spirit. **"And when he had said this, he breathed on them, and saith unto them, Receive ye the Holy Ghost"** (John 20:22). God doesn't intend for you to live for Him on your own; He wants to live through you by the supernatural power of the Holy Spirit!

Jesus was baptized in the Holy Spirit. **"Now when all the people were baptized, it came to pass, that Jesus also being baptized, and praying, the heaven was opened, And the Holy Ghost descended in a bodily shape like a dove upon him, and a voice came from heaven, which said, Thou art my beloved Son; in thee I am well pleased"** (Luke 3:21-22). **"The Spirit of the Lord is upon me, because he hath anointed me to preach the gospel to the poor; he hath sent me to heal the brokenhearted, to preach deliverance to the captives, and recovering of sight to the blind, to set at liberty them that are bruised, To preach the acceptable year of the Lord"** (Luke 4:18-19). If the Son of God Himself needed the Holy Spirit, how much more do we?

The gift of the Holy Spirit comes to all who ask in faith. **"For every one that asketh receiveth; and he that**

seeketh findeth; and to him that knocketh it shall be opened. If a son shall ask bread of any of you that is a father, will he give him a stone? or if he ask a fish, will he for a fish give him a serpent? Or if he shall ask an egg, will he offer him a scorpion? If ye then, being evil, know how to give good gifts unto your children: how much more shall your heavenly Father give the Holy Spirit to them that ask him" (Luke 11:10-13). Your heavenly Father knows how to give you good gifts. Ask Him in faith, and you'll receive the baptism in the Holy Spirit too!

Both Holy Spirit and water baptisms are clearly commanded in the Scriptures. The Lord will lead you into these two acts of faith and obedience as soon as you are born again. Both actions release tremendous benefits into your spiritual life!

For more information, please refer to my in-depth look at the baptism in the Holy Spirit in my book *The Holy Spirit.*

Chapter 5

Build a Sure Foundation

The Bible is God's Word. He'll give you wisdom and guidance through it. **"As newborn babes, desire the sincere milk of the word, that ye may grow thereby"** (1 Pet. 2:2). As a baby draws sustenance from its mother's breast, so a new believer is nourished by spiritual milk from the Bible. You'll grow as you feed often on God's Word!

God's Word is God-breathed. **"All scripture is given by inspiration of God"** (2 Tim. 3:16). The Bible is charged with the very life of God, and it'll come alive to you as you read it. Through His Word, you'll get to know this awesome, loving God who has saved you. You'll grow in the grace and knowledge of Jesus Christ and become **"thoroughly furnished unto all good works"** (2 Tim. 3:17).

God will speak directly to you through the Bible. **"For the word of God is quick, and powerful, and sharper than any twoedged sword, piercing even to the dividing asunder of soul and spirit, and of the joints and marrow, and is a discerner of the thoughts and intents of the heart"** (Heb. 4:12). Don't just use your head to read this book; come to the Word with an open heart ready to receive from God!

Choose a version of the Bible that's easy to understand. God doesn't want language style to hinder you from getting to know Him. Personally, I use the *King James Version* because it's what I grew up on. However, you may find the old English phrases too difficult to understand. If that's the case, then select a Bible to your liking and read, study, and meditate it. Any version you use is superior to not reading the Bible at all. The Holy Spirit can lead you to other translations later on, but laying a solid foundation of God's Word in your heart is what's most important right now!

God's Word—The Highest Authority

A basic understanding of the Bible is very helpful. I never went to seminary or Bible school, but I started studying the Bible sixteen hours a day, and it revolutionized my life! Some things I learned right away; others took me many years. But you can never exhaust the depths of God's Word. Everything you need for life and godliness can be found in it!

I wish somebody had explained to me the difference between the Old Covenant (Genesis through Malachi) and the New Covenant (Matthew through Revelation) when I was first saved. It took me a long time to discover that God deals with people totally differently from one covenant to the other. Most Christians see the Bible as one unit, all saying the same thing. They can't comprehend why the same God shows so much wrath and judgment in the Old Testament and so much grace and mercy in the New. They don't realize how everything changed between God and man once Jesus Christ came to earth. You and I are in the New Covenant in Christ Jesus!

Guidance from mature believers can save you time and painful mistakes, but always check it against God's Word for yourself. Be careful only to receive what's right, because people can steer you in the wrong direction. That's why comparing everything they say with the Bible to see how it matches up is so important. Let go of what doesn't line up, and hold on to what does. God's Word must be the highest authority in your life!

The Word of God is powerful! It's not just a book written by man about God. Some people raise questions about the Bible and say there are many inconsistencies within it. Many good books (called "apologetics") answer these questions and validate the authority of the Bible. The Word is actually a book by God speaking to you through man. All the books in the Bible are supernaturally inspired and have been protected and preserved error free. Your job is to interpret and believe God's Word as it was written. If you do, God Himself will fellowship with you—and that's awesome!

My teaching *A Sure Foundation* will help you understand how important God's Word is to your life.

Chapter 6

Join a Local Church

Every step I've mentioned so far—being water baptized, receiving the baptism in the Holy Spirit, building a sure foundation in the Word of God—can be made much easier if you get involved in a good local church.

The Lord created the church, which is simply a group of His people who meet together regularly for the purpose of loving each other, praying for each other, and building each other up. It doesn't always function that way, but it's still the greatest institution on earth!

Many people love the Lord but don't like His people. That's because some Christians don't reflect God like they should. They hurt others with their mean-spiritedness and hypocrisy. Jesus faced the same thing—unbelievers welcomed Him, while religious folks persecuted Him. Because of this, you may want to commit your life to Christ and enjoy a relationship with Him but have nothing to do with a church. I can relate to what you're feeling, but that's a wrong attitude to keep. It's like fixing a leaky boat—better to be inside making repairs than outside in the ocean where you could drown!

Coals Stay Hot in the Fire

You grow spiritually by participating in a good church. As a believer, you're like a hot coal in a burning fire. You'll stay red hot and glowing as long as you're involved with other believers in a local church body. Separate and isolate yourself from the other coals, and it won't be long before you grow cold. Stay in the fire! Although there are plenty of bad churches out there, it's worth your effort to find the good ones. Every believer needs to be involved in a local church!

You can learn a lot from other Christians who have walked in God's Word and been through some things. It's important not to believe just anyone, but God will place spiritual leaders in your life for the purpose of helping you grow. **"And he gave some, apostles; and some, prophets; and some, evangelists; and some, pastors and teachers; For the perfecting of the saints, for the work of the ministry, for the edifying of the body of Christ"** (Eph. 4:11-12). Many new believers want to bypass people and receive everything they need straight from God. However, the Lord prefers to work through mature Christians to build up and strengthen newer ones.

God uses apostles, prophets, evangelists, pastors, and teachers to equip and mature believers for the work of the ministry. He gave these people to build up the body of Christ until **"we all come in the unity of the faith, and of the knowledge of the Son of God, unto a perfect man, unto the measure of the stature of the fulness of Christ"** (Eph. 4:13). Since the church hasn't fully attained that yet, God is still using these five different types of ministry gifts to accomplish His goals. It's important that you submit to the Lord's system!

You are disobeying God if you don't get involved with other believers. God will still love you and you won't lose your salvation, but you'll be a cold, isolated coal when you run into hurts and difficult situations. Instead of having a strong support system of other believers who love you and know your situation, you'll be on your own in the ocean. You definitely need to participate in a good church!

Relationship with His People

What you hear while you're young in the Lord will greatly impact your spiritual development. As a new believer, you're like a little plant that needs to be in a protected environment until your roots grow deep. When I was young in my faith, I'd walk out in the middle of a service if I heard something contrary to God's Word being preached. Today, I don't just get up and leave, because I know it won't hurt me the way it would've when I was first born again. However, I don't subject myself to wrong teaching again and again, because it's unwise. If you hear something enough you'll start to believe it. Since you are forming your spiritual root structures, it's crucial that you hear right teaching now.

Although what you hear as a new believer is important, a church will supply you with more than just teaching. Your participation in a local body can provide you with needed fellowship and relationships with other Christians. Media ministries like mine can feed you God's Word through audio messages, books, websites, radio, and television programs, but nothing helps the Word become flesh in your life better than regular interaction with other on-fire believers!

Christianity is a relationship with God and His people. Before his conversion, Paul (then named Saul) hated Christians. While on his way to Damascus to kill more believers, the Lord appeared to him in a blinding flash of light (Acts 9:1-5). Jesus asked, "Why are you persecuting Me?" Notice that His question wasn't, "Why are you persecuting My people?" That's because the Lord becomes one with every individual who puts his or her faith in Him! If someone touches you, they touch the apple of God's eye. God loves you the same as He loves every other Christian!

God demonstrates His love through His people. **"By this shall all men know that ye are my disciples, if ye have love one to another"** (John 13:35). **"If a man say, I love God, and hateth his brother, he is a liar: for he that loveth not his brother whom he hath seen, how can he love God whom he hath not seen"** (1 John 4:20). No one who refuses to relate to God's people can say they truly have a relationship with God.

Put His Word into Practice

A local church will provide you with the opportunity to put Christ's teachings into practice. It's one thing to hear the Word say to do unto others as you would have them do unto you (Matt. 7:12), but it's quite another to actually live it. Your rate of maturity will slow down if all you ever do is shut yourself up with a Bible for weeks and months. Some things you'll never really learn until you have to deal with other people. From God's perspective, you don't really know something from His Word until you've put it into practice!

Your local church leadership can provide ministry to you and your loved ones in practical ways that a media/traveling ministry cannot. I can teach you God's Word concerning healing, but I won't be available when you need to **"call for the elders of the church"** to come over to your house and anoint the sick (James 5:14). However, the leaders of your local church can do that and so much more! They can officiate weddings, perform funerals, minister to your children, advise you from the Word, pray about specific situations, and serve as godly role models you can personally interact with on a regular basis. Your entire household will benefit from your participation in a local church!

You'll also find like-minded believers with whom you can establish close friendships. The two most important influences in your life are what you hear/read and with whom you spend your time. This doesn't mean you reject people who aren't believers, but from now on, your strongest friendships should be with other Christians (2 Cor. 6:14-18). If you remain unequally yoked with an unbeliever, sooner or later that person will negatively affect you. **"He that walketh with wise men shall be wise: but a companion of fools shall be destroyed"** (Prov.13:20). You always rise or sink to the level of your closest friends!

Regularly meeting together with other believers protects and promotes your spiritual health. **"Let us hold fast the profession of our faith without wavering; (for he is faithful that promised;) And let us consider one another to provoke unto love and to good works: Not forsaking the assembling of ourselves together, as the manner of some is; but exhorting one another: and so much the more, as ye see the day approaching"** (Heb. 10:23-25). Plug yourself into a good local church!

Find a Good Church

Don't let minor doctrinal issues prevent you from settling into a good church. If the differences are just some external matters and not core beliefs, I suggest you stay involved. Even if it's not a strong faith-teaching church, it's better to participate in some local church than none at all, because of the other important benefits you gain. If you live in an area where you have a choice, always choose a church that preaches the whole counsel of God!

A good church preaches everything God offers in His Word—salvation, baptism in the Holy Spirit, the gifts of the Spirit, healing, deliverance, and prosperity! The denomination I grew up in centered all of the preaching on just the forgiveness of sins. Many people (like me) got saved, but they didn't believe that God's miraculous power was for today. When my father (a leader in that church) became seriously ill, my family and I didn't know how to receive healing from the Lord. No one in our church had faith for it because we were never taught healing from God's Word. My father died at 54 years of age, leaving me fatherless at 12 and my mother a widow at 38. Much pain came into our lives as a result of this. Our church didn't cause this problem, but it sure didn't equip us to overcome it either!

Be part of a church that teaches the whole counsel of God. Don't stay somewhere that's against the baptism in the Holy Spirit, the gifts of the Holy Spirit, healing, and so on. Having your name on a pew or your aunt as the choir director won't help when you're sick. Although you're personally aware that God heals, you'll be frustrated when you have trouble receiving it, because you don't know God's Word. To receive prosperity, deliverance, or whatever, you need to be taught God's Word. Be part of a church you can wholeheartedly support!

A good church preaches faith and grace for the entire Christian life, not just forgiveness of your sins. Many groups teach that all you need to do to initially receive is believe, but that after you're saved, everything is based on your performance. That's wrong! You don't have to earn God's favor, earn answers to prayer, earn God's love, earn your healing, or earn anything else. Everything God gives you is by grace through faith!

The atmosphere ought to encourage healthy relationships. The pastor should set the tone by being a loving person. It's not necessarily better to go to a big church or a small one. Some big churches have small groups for the purpose of nurturing and maturing believers. Often, small churches naturally have an environment conducive to building friendships and spiritual growth. Whether big or small, your experience in a church will normally come down to the quality of your relationships there.

Trust the Lord to lead you to a good local church. Pray, then take some steps of faith. It's His good pleasure to guide you to your place in His body!

Chapter 7

Know Him Intimately

God saved you for the purpose of enjoying an intimate relationship with Him from now on! Salvation isn't just "insurance" from hell's flames. Neither does God intend that you receive forgiveness for your sins and then merely survive until heaven. Salvation is so much more! **"For God so loved the world, that he gave his only begotten Son, that whosoever believeth in him should not perish, but have everlasting life"** (John 3:16). **"And this is life eternal, that they might know thee the only true God, and Jesus Christ, whom thou hast sent"** (John 17:3). Salvation is getting to know this awesome, wonderful, loving God for the rest of eternity!

Jesus came to give you eternal life. The idea that salvation is merely "fire insurance" came from the church putting a period where the Bible only has a comma. It's not **"For God so loved the world, that he gave his only begotten Son, that whosoever believeth in him should not perish"** period. So many preachers stop here and emphasize salvation's byproduct of missing hell and totally ignore God's primary purpose—**"but have everlasting life."** You were saved for intimate relationship with your heavenly Father and His Son!

Jesus came because He loved you! He didn't come as a dutiful Creator under some sense of obligation to rescue His wayward creation. Christ's motivation was pure love, and anyone who loves has a need to be loved in return! God's compassion for you in your lost condition and His passion to restore you to fellowship with Him was combined into a sacrificial love that endured the cross. With the barrier of sin forever removed, you've been freed to receive His love and love Him in return!

The relationship Adam and Eve lost has now been restored to you. **"Who gave himself for our sins, that he might deliver us from this present evil world, according to the will of God and our Father"** (Gal. 1:4). Jesus didn't just save you from a future evil world (hell); He also delivered you from this present evil world according to the Father's will. You are now able to walk and talk with Him!

Get to know God! **"Thou wilt shew me the path of life: in thy presence is fulness of joy; at thy right hand**

there are pleasures for evermore" (Ps. 16:11). **"Jesus Christ: Whom having not seen, ye love; in whom, though now ye see him not, yet believing, ye rejoice with joy unspeakable and full of glory"** (1 Pet. 1:7-8). True joy and happiness in this life come from your intimacy with God. Knowing Him is eternal life!

Follow Me

Become a disciple of the Lord Jesus Christ! A "disciple" is a learner, someone who follows another. **"If ye continue in my word, then are ye my disciples indeed; And ye shall know the truth, and the truth shall make you free"** (John 8:31-32). Learn what God's Word says, and do what He instructs you to do. As you step out in faith to follow Jesus, the freedom in your life will increase more and more!

Your heart attitude should be *Lord, I know You love me, and I love You too. Show me what to do and I'll do it! I follow You!* Lay everything out before Him and make no reservations. Recognize that He is God and you're not. Hold nothing back from Him because He's already given you everything—He laid down His very life for you!

The truth shall make you free. **"Thy word is truth"** (John 17:17). It's only the Word you know and follow that makes you free. You can carry your Bible under your arm and set it beside your bed, but until you put His Word in your heart, it won't do you any good. Meditate (chew on)

His Word until it becomes a part of you. Once you believe it to the point of taking action, you'll know that Word intimately. When this knowledge comes, it'll set you free!

I strongly suggest you get my teaching "Eternal Life." It expounds much more on your relationship with the Lord.

You've Chosen Wisely

Welcome to God's family! If you take to heart what I've shared with you and do it, you'll be well on your way to maturity.

I've included for you a helpful list of teaching materials available that discuss in much greater detail many of the topics I touched on in this book (see "***Helpful Materials***"). God will use them to further deepen your roots and strengthen your foundation. I strongly encourage you to get ahold of them as soon as possible!

Choosing to make the Lord Jesus Christ the center of your life is the greatest decision you'll ever make! I congratulate you for choosing wisely. As your brother in Christ, I wish to leave you with this Word from God our Father: **"But grow in grace, and in the knowledge of our Lord and Saviour Jesus Christ. To him be glory both now and for ever. Amen"** (2 Pet. 3:18).

Receiving Jesus as your Savior

Choosing to receive Jesus Christ as your Lord and Savior is the most important decision you'll ever make!

God's Word promises **"that if thou shalt confess with thy mouth the Lord Jesus, and shalt believe in thine heart that God hath raised him from the dead, thou shalt be saved. For with the heart man believeth unto righteousness; and with the mouth confession is made unto salvation"** (Rom. 10:9-10). **"For whosoever shall call upon the name of the Lord shall be saved"** (Rom. 10:13).

By His grace, God has already done everything to provide salvation. Your part is simply to believe and receive.

Pray out loud, ***"Jesus, I confess that You are my Lord and Savior. I believe in my heart that God raised You from the dead. By faith in Your Word, I receive salvation now. Thank You for saving me!"***

The very moment you commit your life to Jesus Christ, the truth of His Word instantly comes to pass in your spirit. Now that you're born again, there's a brand-new you!

Receiving the Holy Spirit

As His child, your loving heavenly Father wants to give you the supernatural power you need to live this new life.

"For every one that asketh receiveth; and he that seeketh findeth; and to him that knocketh it shall be opened...how much more shall your heavenly Father give the Holy Spirit to them that ask him" (Luke 11:10,13).

All you have to do is ask, believe, and receive!

Pray, ***"Father, I recognize my need for Your power to live this new life. Please fill me with Your Holy Spirit. By faith, I receive it right now! Thank You for baptizing me! Holy Spirit, You are welcome in my life!"***

Congratulations—now you're filled with God's supernatural power!

Some syllables from a language you don't recognize will rise up from your heart to your mouth (1 Cor. 14:14). As you speak them out loud by faith, you're releasing God's power from within and building yourself up in the spirit (1 Cor. 14:4). You can do this whenever and wherever you like!

It doesn't really matter whether you felt anything or not when you prayed to receive the Lord and His Spirit. If you believed in your heart that you received, then God's Word promises you did. **"Therefore I say unto you, What things soever ye desire, when ye pray, believe that ye receive them, and ye shall have them"** (Mark 11:24). God always honors His Word. Believe it!

Please contact me and let me know that you've prayed to receive Jesus as your Savior or be filled with the Holy Spirit. I would like to rejoice with you and help you understand more fully what has taken place in your life. I'll send you a free gift that will help you understand and grow in your new relationship with the Lord. *"Welcome to your new life!"*

Recommended Materials

Spirit, Soul & Body

Understanding the relationship of your spirit, soul, and body is foundational to your Christian life. You will never truly know how much God loves you or believe what His Word says about you until you do. Learn how they're related and how that knowledge will release the life of your spirit into your body and soul. It may even explain why many things are not working the way you had hoped.

Item Code: 1027 4-Tape album
Item Code: 1027-C 4-CD album
Item Code: 318 Paperback

Eternal Life

Is eternal life just about living forever, or could there be more? What does God's Word say? Andrew's answer to this question may change the way you view salvation and your approach to your relationship with God. This single teaching is the first from the *Introducing Discipleship Evangelism* album.

Item Code: DE01 Single Tape
Item Code: DE01-C Single CD

Water Baptism

What is water baptism all about? What really happens when you get baptized? How should it be done? These are just a few of the questions Don Krow will answer from the Word of God concerning baptism.

Item Code: 67K Single Tape

A Sure Foundation

God's Word is the only true foundation for your life. Listen as Andrew explains the supernatural process that occurs when you plant the Word in your heart. He uses the example of how Jesus dealt with John the Baptist's unbelief to reveal the power of the Word.

Item Code: 1034 4-Tape album

The True Nature Of God

Are you confused about the nature of God? Is He the God of judgment found in the Old Testament or the God of mercy and grace found in the New Testament? Andrew's revelation on this subject will set you free and give you a confidence in your relationship with God like never before. This is truly nearly-too-good-to-be-true news.

Item Code: 1002 3-Tape album
Item Code: 1002-C 3-CD album
Item Code: 308 Paperback

You've Already Got It

Are you trying to get the Lord to heal, bless, deliver, or prosper you? If so, stop it! God has already done all he will ever do for you. How can that be? Listen as Andrew teaches on the balance between grace and faith, and you'll understand you've already got what you need. Never again will you beg God for anything.

Item Code: 1033 6-Tape album
Item Code: 1033-C 6-CD album

Introducing Discipleship Evangelism

Did God call us to make converts or disciples? It's an important question. The misunderstanding of that has led to some appalling statistics. Many evangelists now realize that only about 15 percent of those who accept Jesus continue in the faith. It's time we changed our thinking and started practicing what Jesus taught. Learn more in this enlightening series.

Item Code: 1028 3-Tape album
Item Code: 1028-C 3-CD album

Contact Information

Andrew Wommack Ministries
P.O. Box 3333
Colorado Springs, CO 80934
Helpline Phone: 719-635-1111
website: www.awmi.net

Andrew Wommack Ministries of Europe
P.O. Box 4392
Walsall WS1 9AR
England
Helpline Phone: +44 (0) 1922 473 300
website: www.awme.net